The Happy Mistress
Volume II
Secrets of a Happy Wife

Noella Fe

Copyright 2018, 2019 by SistaLadiFriend Publishing
Company.
New York, NY 10016
The Happy Mistress Volume II
Secrets of a Happy Wife
Written by, Author
Edited by, Author; C. Green; J.M. Lee
ISBN: 978-1-7321983-4-0

"It is queer when one sits back and thinks, I've chosen to be someone's wife. A sudden rush clusters your skin and you become warm with the idea that this is love. For it is the same queer hot flustering feeling when you are angered, that you are the wife."
-Noella Fe

Acknowledgments and Thank you

Of course, I thank Allah and the universe he sustains. Of course, he created me, but most of all, I want to send a big thank you to the person who made me a wife, my *Mista. I mean I couldn't '*talk my talk' if It wasn't for him! May Allah give you the *deep-throat wife you deserve.
(hahahahhahhahahh)
Ok, Okay. I tried to be serious but when have you known me to follow all the way thru a conversation without a good laugh or two? (slaps thigh) WHEW! That was funny!
I dedicate this book to every current wife, every future wife and every woman that has hopes of becoming married. Don't take this little book as a, 'What to do type of book.' Look at it as (looks to the heavens) wife talk! I want to show the positive side of dealing with the reality of being a wife. I don't promote happiness thru sadness. I value and live by self care, self worth and keeping it one thousand times infinite with myself. I ALSO DON'T PROMOTE *WIFEISM THROUGH VANITY.
I want to give a special acknowledgment to those women that weather the storm and those that no matter how it ended they understood it was simply the end of a chapter in their lives. Once a wife, always wife material, remember that.

4

I want to give acknowledgment to the wives who are still trying to figure it out; it's not easy baby, god bless you! Just read the book, you'll laugh, you'll think and maybe just maybe it will help your wife life.

And of course, this is dedicated to and for all the dam wives that can't get it together! Be a reflection of what you want in your marriage!

Let me acknowledge all the great people I met through the first book; I appreciate your energy.

To the greats that I worked with; I appreciate your creativity.

To all the wonderful authors I have come across; I appreciate your vibe and blessings. Let's continue to support each other and create magic for the world.

I want to acknowledge, Chante Graham as well. She was a vessel that helped The HAPPY MISTRESS go way beyond my TV expectations in such a short amount of time. I learned a lot. I wish you nothing but success my sister. May Allah grant you all your heart desires.

Last but most important, to my current and future audience. THANK YOU from the bottom of my stinky little heart! The good the bad and the ugly; the wait···. the wait··· wait the wait... Your patience I truly appreciate!

Thank you for your inquiries, concerns, your love and all that good energy; keep it coming.

SECRETS OF
A
HAPPY WIFE

DISCLAIMER

Even though many of you are used to my style of writing, there are new readers. Therefore, I have to put this out there.

I am mainly discussing me and my experiences. I was married for almost 20 years without being 'cheated' on and without ever regretting my decision to become a wife. I think I can give a little advice to others. I do reference other married individuals. I even share letters from married couples in some chapters, but identities are hidden. Don't PUT YOUR BUSINESS OUT THERE OFF OF SPECULATION THAT THIS BOOK IS ABOUT YOU. IT'S NOT. I changed some names and switched a couple of things up because everything in the book is written based on true events and I do respect the privacy of others.

I won't purposely offend anyone, race, creed or color, religion, etc. However, I will state my opinion. MY MATERIAL HAS NEVER BEEN FOR THE SENSITIVE. It's for the mature. The curious and those with a good sense of humor about this thing called life.

PREFACE

Here we are again! It's been a while since I sat down to converse about married folk business hasn't it? Something baffling happened though! An A-Lister's wife came out and said on her very popular show, that the first time she was happy in her marriage was in August 2019.(wrinkles face) I said, "Oh boy, lemme put this dam book out; they out there trying to fool the people again." Plus, I've been sitting on it for like 3 years waiting patiently and boom the lord said NOW. I hope it was the lord. (shrugs)

The last book, Secrets of a Happy Mistress stirred a lot of pots. Celebrities and locals had a lot to say, but guess what? I have wayyy more to say. I received so many emails asking for visuals or receipts about my actual affairs. If you were paying close attention to the 'wave I ride' you would know that I would never disclose my lovers. Sorry, that book wasn't that. I didn't need to give you visuals, Hollyhood did that for me.

I received a lot of mail downplaying the book saying there weren't any secrets in the book; Well dearies that's the secret in itself. I had nothing to gain by breaking trust or hearts. That's the problem with some of you now, you gotta know too much about someone else's business to move accordingly in your own affairs. The things you should research you don't and the *gems that are given to you, you deny them because you don't or can't see the value in it right away. The value comes from you. That book nor this book is going to tell you how to live your life. My little books are written to make you think about the many options in this world that you can choose from and being content and confident in your decisions.

Readers and authors alike wanted the second & third book to be like a novel and they wanted them out asap. I couldn't do it. I didn't want to. THE HAPPY MISTRESS had to stand on her own to make my point and it did, many points I might add. There are levels to the lifestyle of the married and happy. I said it in my first book, *more wives knowest than not*. I needed Hollyhood & locals alike to do the footwork while I lay the groundwork for my series. Funny thing eh, as I was putting the finishing touches on this book, a favorite daytime gossip show-host FINALLYYYY, admitted- oops I mean revealed to the world that indeed her husband had a mistress. HER STATEMENT: She wasn't going anywhere! HER STORY: neither was the ring or her husband.

NOW WHY WOULD YOU NEED ME TO GIVE YOU
RECEIPTS? When clearly you don't need receipts
from anyone else. Plus, all the receipts that come
out usually come out after someone has ran with the
lie for decades. I told you in the first book, some
wives get married to stay married. No matter what,
this superwoman said she isn't even considering
divorce. Let's see if she sticks with her story. How
You Doin? (in my Wendy Williams voice).
Raises eyebrow and sips...

Secrets of a Happy Mistress was not about how to
be a mistress; You had to exist as a mistress
already. I made that very clear in my first book.
Even though many chose to see it as a bunch of
nonsense that didn't apply to them, you didn't have
to be a mistress to apply the secrets. You just had
to be married or a Mistress to understand the book.
I gave you differences between a homewrecker,
mistress & a side chick along with the
consequences of being a homewrecker. NOT A
MISTRESS.

The facts were written! I laid it out what could happen and what would happen if you got caught up as a mistress! I could not tell you how many women hit me up saying that my book didn't tell them shit. (Sips and blinks) To those women, you were looking for me to tell you it was ok for you to do what you were doing; you were looking for juicy scandalous ways to be this illuminating seductress. To those women, you need therapy and a fucking hug.

(How many IG models were on top of the world with one of the A-listers just to fall from grace because she forgot she had surgery and the britches she was stepping into was too big for her. (That might go over a lot of heads). Simple, she thought she was going to replace the wife!

The messages in this book will sound very similar to Volume One. 'Only a married man can make a woman a mistress.' Too many women were misspeaking about their 'title.' Understand there can be many girlfriends, side chicks, and main chicks that think they're the only woman, but there is only one wife. The message is similar, 'Only a husband can make you a wife.' In this book, the 'titles' are switched and the focus is on the most important part of the marriage, THE WIFE.

Before my first book came out, millionaires were not discussing the infidelity in their marriage. These things were flat out denied. Now you have mainstream artist breaking down talking about their own marital problems and making money off of the public at the same time. TRENDY, isn't it?

I spent many social media hours going back and forth telling people (females mostly) that their most adored celebrity allows her man to step out ANDDD she's eating ass. (Shrugs) My book proved wives wanna stay married. THE HAPPY MISTRESS also proved that no matter what, some women don't marry to get divorced.

Mrs. Harris, I luvvvvv me some Mrs. Harris. (Rapper, T.I.'s wife) proved that to you.

This book is mainly for the new wives, the already wives. However, it could be a good tool for someone who eventually would like to walk down the aisle. You know, like a starter kit, eh.

INTRO

YOU WILL NOT UNDERSTAND ANY LEVEL OF
THIS BOOK IF YOU ARE NOT MARRIED.
IF YOU ARE GOING TO GET MARRIED THIS BOOK
WILL HELP YOU GATHER YOURSELF BEFORE
YOU COMMIT.
IF YOU ARE NEITHER MARRIED OR
WAITING/WANTING TO GET MARRIED, JUST
READ THE BOOK FOR THE LOVE OF GOD AND
KEEP IT AS A CONVERSATION PIECE! lol

Just like everyone became *woke and connected to
the ancestors, now everyone is a marriage
counselor. QUITE THE TREND, isn't it?
The funny part to me is, many of these counselors,
aren't married, were never married, or have failed
marriages. Talk shows dedicated precious time
telling worn-out women and timid men the best way
to maneuver a marriage void of cheating. Not many
actually broke down the individual, the couple, or
the union. You had an abundance of men telling
women how to be women, and too many women
telling women how to be men. (Raises eyebrows)

This book is not meant to shade or down anyone that isn't living their best *wife life*. It's not a book glorifying married women; WELLLL, it is a celebration of wives tho. This is not a book condemning any one way some women choose to carry out their married duties. This book is simply for those that take marriage seriously, but most of all, this book is for wives that take themselves seriously.

 Just as I didn't give you any juice on my mistress affairs, I won't give much on my marriage. Not because I'm being candid, but aren't you tired of looking at an original piece and trying to either have it or something like it when in reality you could be creating your own peace and have something customized to you and your husband? (I meant to spell peace the way I did.)

I purposely wrote the books in this order. If I had put everything in one book at one time, you would have missed these gems I'm about to drop. Now like I said anyone could read this, but I'm talking directly to women that are married. I'm talking to the woman that chose to be a wife.

It's time you chop it up with Noella Fe, on a different level. I am, was, and still is a wife! (lol) Before you ask, I was a wife before I was a Mistress and I remained a wife after. YUP! You guessed it! Noella Fe was successful at both. LOLOLOLOL (sips)

So, forget the mainstream advisors that had to go through hell to find heaven. Kick back and chat with someone who created her own lanes, was happy in them and had no problem making new lanes when it was time.

Get your wine, coffee, *Patron or *D'USSE. Grab your notepad, pen or highlighter! I know you all are going to have plenty of questions, comments, concerns, threats, and insults. lollop. It's time to jump back into my world. I bet this time around you'll be ready. (wink)

My husband never cheated on me. For that to have occurred that would have meant I cheated myself.
−Noella Fe

SECRETS TO A HAPPY WIFE....

WHERE TO FIND NOELLA FE

There was never a day I didn't want to be a wife. There were no days I wished I was someone else's wife and there were no days I regret choosing to be a wife; regardless of how I became one.
—Noella Fe

1
HOW DID I GET HERE?
Recognize why you wanted to become a wife.

Too many women just look at the fairytale part of marriage. Hell, plenty women don't think past the wedding day! Have you ever met a woman who didn't even think about her honeymoon? I have. On my blog I often share emails that I receive from all types of scenarios. The worst scenario is the woman that never thought about the true reasons she became married. There are women who do not think past the wedding, it's instantly an "I" situation and that is the type of woman that has to get adjusted to wife life.

MAIL TIME!

Dear Noella Fe,

I just read your book 'Secrets of a Happy Mistress' good read. One thing I can say is, I never thought about a mistress. I also follow your periscope. You are very honest about why you got married, you make fun of you and your husband and I often find myself wanting something similar. Anyway, I never really thought about why I got married as how you say. I just wanted to get married because every girl wants to walk down the aisle, right?

Well a couple of years later this is not what I want to be doing, I feel like I could have stayed the way we were before. We played house; it was just like marriage. Things have drastically changed, so thanks to you; today I admitted to myself that I got married for the superficial part. I'm not sure if he feels the same way, I'm not sure of anything, what do you suggest?

newly married and miserable

What I suggested after some questions are this,

MY RESPONSE

"*If there is trust then you can discuss your doubts as a wife with your husband.*" Marriage is not like dating and when YOU realize that, the next step is to tackle the challenges your going to face as a wife. If you still want to be one. I CAN NOT STRESS ENOUGH, YOU HAVE TO KNOW WHAT YOU WANT. You need to know the difference between, marriage isn't for me versus marriage is so different for me. One can be worked on and fixed, the other cannot.

Noella Fe

Honeyyyyy, y'all got to do better! One thing I did early on, I never forgot why I got married. (FIRST STEP TO THIS SECRET IS KEEP IT REAL WITH YOURSELF AND THEN YOUR PARTNER AS TO WHY YOU GOT MARRIED.) It made my life simple to a great extent on those trying days. I kept myself grounded with the reasons and benefits of my decisions.

Ok, *'Miss I want a husband'.* What made you want to be a wife? Why did you get married? Why do you want to get married? I went around town asking these questions and many had the same answer; *"I want someone to grow old with··· to love", to-* blah blah freakin blah. (I almost cursed) Nobody ever says, *"because I wanted fame or fortune or a safety net."* Not one person I know in real or fake life, ever admitted to getting married for a lifelong fucking partner they could sex raw anytime they wanted. No one says, because of vengeance (getting married to spite someone). No woman ever says OPENLY, *"because I got pregnant AND this is me saving face for my family."* I'm not even shocked at how many women don't want to be wives let alone being married. It could be because they were raised that way. We have all seen it before; everybody in the whole family married by 14 (rolls eyes and sighs). Those are what I call generational marriages. Those work for the most part and divorce is usually never an option. HAHA, therapy isn't an option either those marriages usually keep their problems secret, and the elders give the advice. (I could be getting this confused with mob hits, but it sounds about right).

The first step you must take is, figuring out why you want to be a wife. Not who wants you to be a wife.

I don't know about you but the narcissist in me refused to be ashamed or regret any decision I have ever made in my life. In my football shaped head everything I ever did turned out great. Even though my marriage was based on business, what kept me grounded was the fact that I chose to be a wife. Simple.

Mail time!

Dear Noella Fe,

Me and my wife have been together for about five years now, when we first got married, she seemed really excited about being married and becoming a mom. My wife always said she wanted kids you know regular stuff. We had planned to have a baby once we relocated; well that has been two years. Every time I bring up the topic of kids she shies away from the conversation. Last month I found out she has been on birth control. I feel like, I'm not sure, but it's messing with me. I have so many thoughts. Should I say-or rather how do I tell her I know? Do I even say anything?
_married waiting on baby.

This is what I wanted to say:

"Do you have thoughts of suicide or thoughts of hurting yourself? It's ok to live and I hope you are not dying over this bull-" ... Sorry! That's what the prompt says when you call the crisis line. Well not the last part but···

But seriously, if you're having an issue being married and your going bat shit crazy, call the crisis line! I wanted to say, "You're at a premature stage in your marriage, if the bitch doesn't want kids either talk it out or walk it out sir, you too deserve happiness.

I didn't say any of that of course! It would have been insensitive for me to do so. I only become insensitive after you become a client. (smile)

My response,

You need to confront your wife.
Too many secrets already. Open the floor just in case she doesn't know how to start the conversation. Express yourself clearly and honestly! You are the one that has been betrayed. This is your chance to get it all out break down, cry and then listen to your wife. Open your mind to hear and understand her, only then can you make a solid decision about your union. Don't pressure yourself or your wife if the end result doesn't add up to everyone equally yoked, satisfied & happy! Good Luck!

Noella Fe

That was for him, but the following advice sweetheart is for you. YOU MARRIED NOW! Babies come with the territory, however, make it clear if you don't want kids. THAT SHOULD HAVE ALREADY BEEN TALKED ABOUT! Save your hubby the heartache. Plus, there are many options besides having to carry one. Surrogacy isn't taboo anymore.

Be honest. Be upfront. What's the worst thing that can happen; you not being marriage material for THAT man? Your move sweetie but marriage is nothing but a big compromise. It's a pull and tug type thing. There's nothing more pitiful than a man wanting babies and the female saying she can't have any knowing damn well her nickname used to be fertile myrtle! Hmmm hmmm breaks my heart. It's even sadder when these types of games are played with innocent hearts and children suffer in the end. It's your body but honestly some of it is your husbands too. If you know that a big chunk of your marriage was/is based on babies; gurlllfrenn, you have some thinking to do and a conversation to be had with your hubby. Do not have babies and you don't want babies those are the children that suffer in the statement I made above.

Marriage is just another game of life. Many don't like to view life as a game, but it is, it's nonexistence if you think about it. However, if you plan to play, play to win, be confident in your decision to be someone's wife. FOR THE PEOPLE WHO NEED THE GEMS TO SHINE, SECRET ONE KNOW WHY YOU WANT TO BECOME OR WHY YOU BECAME A WIFE. When all you want to be is married, a lot of problems arise.

As with anything in life never compare your grass to the neighbors. By this time, you know only fake grass stays green all year around.
−Noella Fe

2
START ACTING LIKE A WIFE AND STOP THINKING LIKE A GIRLFRIEND

I like looking at social media to see when all the baby mama's and girlfriends of the world start talking shit about a celebrity post concerning their marital issues. I really like when the mistress steps outta pocket only to be made a fool of by wife and THE HUSBAND. "Oh, when I get married" is the tagline. SMH. It's really the highlight of my life. It's typical girlfriend behavior to speak on another woman's shit knowing her yard is full of human feces.(wrinkles face) You have got to know why you got married because that is really going to determine what type of wife you are or will be. Once you get married you no longer should be thinking like you still have to leave his house in the morning. Or lowering your own energy because you are unsure exactly where you fit in. This is also very important for you to figure out why you are married, so you can act accordingly, no matter the situation.

MAIL TIME!

Dear Noella Fe says,

My husband has been acting really funny lately. I don't want to ask him directly, then he might feel I'm annoying or invading his privacy. What should I do?

questions

My Response

Simply put, be willing to observe what you're unwilling to ask. I must insert this bit of advice though; YOU are a wife and shouldn't feel like you can't ask your husband what's ailing him. It's time to admit YOU are the one who is having an issue here. You actually don't know if he is acting funny or if something is truly wrong. Closed mouth doesn't get fed.

Noella Fe

See, in the Secrets of a Happy Mistress; I explained to you the mistress has no place or business asking her married man shit about his life. But you're not her, you're the wife. Honey you have got to take control of your title and role, don't half step! Once you are a wife you no longer have to be in girlfriend mode, creeping and sneaking for information. Getting migraines from assuming shit, enough already! Ask questions! No such thing as being annoying to your husband. If you're annoying then either someone was faking (probably you), not being themselves or maybe you guys shouldn't be married. SHRUGS. If you're annoying your husband knows baby girl, he likes it believe me that's why he married you. (smile)

Annoying habits have nothing to do with communication. Maybe the deliverance, but never the direct act of communicating. You're married. Girlfriends talk at their men because they think they aren't listening. As a wife you can talk to your husband because you KNOW he's listening. Comb through the flaws and create something magical. There is no room for timidness. Now, if you are scared to be you then maybe you are not the wife for your husband. Furthermore, ask yourself if this a real fear and why. There is a major difference than being scared to talk to your husband versus a mixed-up communication line. Fear is for those on the outside of the house, not the occupants inside. Girlfriends hold their tongue in the belief that holding back will keep him. Sorry to break it to you, but as a wife, all that's going to do is give you a complex and set in motion a way of life that, in the end, will be disastrous.

While we are on this chapter of stop thinking like a girlfriend, I have to touch on this note, a lot of things will change including your social life, you should not be looking for single friends to hang with or bring home. This one might shock you especially if you think you one of the bros. As a wife you no longer get to act like a homie, particularly with the singles of your husband's crew. Your husband understands this new level the two of you are on, so should you.

MAIL TIME!

Dear Noella Fe,

Me and my husband got into a big blow up over the fact that he doesn't want me to hang out with him and his *homies anymore. His reasonings to me are for kids, he can't even tell me what has changed so much that I can't be around people that I've been around before. I told him I wouldn't have a problem with him being around me and my friends, I'm just trying to get an understanding did I miss something? So much is changing since we married and moved in together.
_looking for clarity

My Response

Now that you are misses with an "R" you must carry yourself that way. Wives don't hang with their husband's friends unless those friends are married and it's a couples thing. Let me put a battery in your back, if you allow YOUR GIRLFRIENDS to hang around your man, they will get comfortable. Nothing worse than a "friend" sitting in your home when you get off of work, talking about I just stopped by. Knock it off girl! Treat your self, your man and most important your marriage with an assload of respect.
_Noella Fe

Another thing girlfriends do without shame is to hang around everyone because they crave to get in; she wants to be down. On top of, she thinks she'll be able to keep tabs on him this way. Quickly realize your husband will be willing to have your tabs on him. (smile)

Honey realize that people have to show you certain courtesies now! You are no longer a homie, friend, hang out buddy or whatever you thought you once were. Oh yes! Being a wife is serious business. Now that you are chosen, you will have to figure out what single business isn't acceptable in married folks' business. Girlfriends are selfish wives shouldn't be. In short grow up, the little girl games are over. You don't need to hang out with him and his friends anymore, that's above you.

You have a lot of thinking to do after you have decided why you want to be a wife. Your next step is to ask yourself, "Am I ready to grow up and leave the life of messy girlfriends, and nosey mama's out of my business? Are you ready to tell the girls, "not tonight", not because you were asked or told but because you realize, going out every time the phone rings are for people who don't have someone to support mentally, physically and spiritually? Are you ready to stop telling your sexual activities and sharing *dick pics? (Lawd, I pray to black baby Jesus, none of y'all ever showed your man's meat to your homies, can u say, dangerous.) Those phone calls are not meant for married women. JUST IN CASE THE PEOPLE IN THE BACK WITH THE BIG GLASSES DIDN'T SEE, SECRET NUMBER 2, YOU'RE NOT A GIRLFRIEND ANYMORE, ACT LIKE A WIFE

Another thing I must stress, shut up. Girlfriends are really chatty about their dude; wives shouldn't be but turn the page, the next chapter sums one of the golden rules and most sacred secret of all.

I don't know if marriages are made up of fairytales,
I just know I didn't have any nightmares.
–Noella Fe

3
SILENCE IS GOLDEN
"Keep Ur Union Affairs Private"

I laugh when I say this because so many women claim to be so private but in reality, their mouths are bigger than the Nile river. These are the wives that consider their friends and mama apart of the marriage. As I stated in the last chapter, girlfriends are chatty. Wives aren't. Nobody needs to know your business. *STFU. *PERIODT! Some things should never leave your mouth about your husband.

MAIL TIME!

Dear Noella,

Girllll, I am so trying to win my man back right now, my engagement broke off a couple of weeks ago. It all started because we had a little disagreement about discussing bedroom matters with our friends. So i called my best friend and she called him to talk to him about it and find out why he felt the way he was feeling. I only did this because it seems we needed a third party. Now, we never had a problem of getting advice from people before, so I'm not sure what's up or why he got so mad. He said, "that what we discussed and how he felt should have been enough for me to digest what he said" Can you say lost? Then he hit me with, I had a big mouth and told me to keep the ring cause I probably would never get another one.

distraught

Shaking my damn head. This little secret can really
boost your whole married life. Now let me say once
you snag a *three-legged creature (check the back
for verbiage ladies) start practicing the art of
silence immediately. I'm talking about soon as you
meet him even if you don't know if he the one! No
man wants to share a side of him he trusts you with
and then come to find out that your friends know.
WHICH MEANS MAYBE TWO FRIENDS AND
SOMEBODY MAMA KNOW TOO! Never ever go to
anyone but your husband about his feelings or his
vulnerabilities. Do not ever discuss with anyone that
your man likes his ass ate! Seriously, I see that's
quite trendy now too. (Rolls eyes) Not the ass
licking, that's been going on since the stars were
created. I'm talking bout telling it. SHHHHH, I'm
telling you while you busy thinking everyone
laughing with you somebody shouting at you and
ready to lick your husband's ass from ball to the
end of his ass crack.

My Response,

Apart of being married is (drum roll) shutting up about your husband and your union. Listen, forget that nonsense about keeping your mouth closed to keep other females away. You need to keep your mouth shut to keep everyone away. Physically and spiritually. You talking about your problems to others creates problems you didn't even have before. Furthermore, negative thought produces negative action, gossiping about your man never produces good results. Just like you and your man pillow talk so does everyone else.
noella fe

Question, why put the negativity in the air? This goes back to the second chapter; it's time to grow up, my dear. Stop telling your mom shit, stop telling your good girlfriends every little thing about your man. The one thing I did enjoy about being married is privacy. When I was a baby mother it was just like *OMG, everybody has something to say about what I should do, or everyone had a suggestion. I realized they only had so much input because that output came from me. I had given a bow and arrow to everyone to take shots at me. Go figure I was the cause of the death of my relationship that wasn't even formed yet. I also understood after I became married why this secret alone was so important. Those long talks I had with people were also able to happen because no one was a wife; we were all just baby mamas···

As a wife, you will undergo the wearing of many hats besides the wife, that includes problem solver. Most men are secretive, and many men think of most challenges that arise are temporary. Stop getting overly excited about things that don't matter enough to discuss it with your hubby. I honestly am telling you no matter how mad you are, how emotional or intense the subject or matter might be, give every drop of that energy to your spouse. From beginning to end. Don't call your friends up and make premeditated decisions that you know you won't follow thru on. Only you will look silly in the end, even if no one has enough guts to tell you. There's someone who can't wait to throw what you put up with in your face behind your back! Instead of your friends consoling you they will be the first ones to judge you especially if them hoes single. *(tilts head).

Listen I know we have all said to somebody, my man ain't shit. But I want you to try something. How about you don't say that anymore, remember if he isn't shit, you ain't shit either. *SMILE

Do not tell anyone your problems as a miserable wife except the one that is making you feel that way. If it isn't him, then he still deserves to know. The only time this secret shouldn't be applied is when it comes to your Mister. Your hubby does not want to be left out.

Another thing I have to throw in here the main thing you wanna keep to yourself, if you happen to go this route, is your infidelities. Let those dirty secrets ride with you if you aren't willing to disclose them to your husband. If you are stepping out you should always be stepping out with your husband's heart, soul and respect close in spirit. DO NOT SHARE THIS WITH ANYONE. DON'T be the wife that thinks she is out-slicking her husband or that it's cute so you bragging about the ability to carry an affair, baby trust me on this: The same friend that you telling the juice to about your *'histress', will be the same one that becomes your husbands mistress. Never let someone shock your husband with news about you. FOR THE PEOPLE THAT WENT TO THE BATHROOM SECRET THREE IS WHAT GOES ON IN YOUR MARRIAGE STAYS IN YOUR MARRIAGE. Treat your marriage like a Vegas trip, "What happens in Vegas stays in Vegas."

4
STOP THINKING SINGLE AND START ACTING MARRIED

Courtesy is the keyword Hunny bunny.
You should no longer be making breakfast only for yourself or stopping to eat on the way home. I know a lot of you was on your independent woman/sex in the city/single life before the right John came along and are very use to doing things for yourself by yourself. I understand but it's just not you anymore. I think you should start purging some of your single activities during the engagement stage if you aren't already married. Even if you and hubby's life is hectic on the go with no kids, pick your man up a meal on the go too on the way in. Small acts go along way in a man's life. That's a parent thing anyways, reserve that move for when you have kids. I have many married homies that didn't give two middle fingers about they significant other. Like sickening. Little actions like that say big words like I said. Men want the married life too! Okay so you haven't purged your single soul and now your married; MAYBE in the beginning it might take a little adjusting, but your husband should not have to ask you three years later to bring him home something to eat. There is no room for selfishness in a good marriage.

MAIL TIME!

Dear Noella

So, I've been married for less than a year, my husband and I aren't seeing eye to eye. He thinks I'm supposed to clean up after him. I work just like he does; I was taught to clean up after yourself. I didn't sign up for dirty laundry and housework. When I met him, he was a neat freak now I'm like wtf. If anything because of his neatness, I thought for sure he would do all the house cleaning anyway. He gets that shit from his mom she cleans like every day, etc. Not me I'm ready to be independent again.

_not a maid

(laughs hard; This letter had me in tears I dare put the whole email in this short chapter!)

My Response

Some men do clean better than women and if you don't like house cleaning take your money and hire a maid or cleaning service. I understand all the complaints you have but here's the thing, do you have a solution besides giving up over laundry? Is it that you just don't want to clean up his stuff or u don't want to clean anything? Every woman wants a clean house, so I don't think you'll really be willing to live like roommates. That's the road it sounds like your headed. I'm not a fan of divorce but honey if you can't get with it, why continue?

There is no room for laziness as a wife, working or not, balance your life. Also let me throw this in, if you haven't discussed this with your husband then the first step is to bring it up to him, if he is a cleaner then it doesn't sound like he will have a problem either doing his share or doing it all, but you won't know until you open that mouth. Just be ready to decrease your appetite if your adding to his plate.

–Noella Fe

By the way I never got an answer. (shrugs) Ladies, listen you will have to do housework. Some men are very good cleaners, I mean better than a lot of women. I know for I have witnessed it with my own eyes. That's not the issue, all these things are really little. Listen some of ya'll men know you aren't the neatest or cleanest and yet he married your nasty ass. (shrugs) There is someone for everyone remember that.

I liked picking up after my man, idk it was something about his dirty jeans in the middle of the bedroom; it could have been the thought of his big buff ass working hard in that Carolina sun that kept me contempt but it was a pleasure. I didn't feel like a maid at all. I wasn't forced to do anything. Don't get me wrong I don't want to paint a picture of the perfect wife (well I could), but I'll stick with my masterpiece painting of a happy wife. There were plenty of days that I did not, I repeat, I did not clean, nor did I cook but he didn't hold it against me, he held it down. Hell, plenty of days I wasn't there, physically or emotionally. He understood and that strengthen me as a wife. I even remember my husband called his mom cause I went on strike. He did start washing his clothes, but it wasn't because I refused to do it, it was simply because he understood I was a wife, not a slave. Everything and anything can be tried once but when you start acting as if the marriage is a 9-5; it changes the tune of the flow. Nothing should be forced in marriage; each party should want to take care of their spouse inside and out. Stop thinking only about yourself, that way if it happens to end it can't be said that you didn't do things out of sincerity. You won't be mad at yourself either.

I didn't get mad at my husband for anything. Frustrated hell yeah! Communication was the key every step of the way. We dealt with it and when all the cards were dealt, we just started with a fresh pack. We both could take care of ourselves individually, but we had to learn how to take care of each other in our marriage. And boy was it challenging. As a wife once I figured out It was my duty to be problem solver, things ran smoothly. JUST IN CASE, YOU CAN'T HEAR IN THE BACK, SECRET 4, you're NOT SINGLE, SO ACT MARRIED.

I asked the young lady that question because listen you don't have to change what you are used too, in no way am I telling you to completely deny your rights, however if you don't want to do the laundry then you should have a way for it to get done. It sounds crazy, but women should always have their own solutions to whatever it is they are having a problem or issue with. The first years can be challenging if you try to get a 40-year marriage in 5 years after becoming man and wife. NEXTTTT CHAPTERRR.

If something needed to be done, someone did it. Me and my husband never let the titles dictate who should do what. Our roles in our union and to each other were more than just husband and wife.
-Noella Fe

5
GIVE YOURSELF TIME
A MARRIAGE IS FOREVER

DON'T BE A QUITTER, I said it in the last chapter (or was it the one before that, looks to side) little things can be handled. Really anything can be handled; issues creep in; it's how you choose to handle things; like a child, a marriage must be nurtured to grow. Learn how to step back and be still. For once in your life, you are allowed to deal directly with whatever feeling or emotion you have without judgment. I honestly think this is the only safe place free of judgement. You should be confident that you and your partner can weather the storm.

MAIL TIME

Dear Noella,

I luvvv your book, I'm currently dealing with a married man but I'm not sure I want to continue, he complains a lot about him and his wife. I don't think he is the aggressive type so when they get in an argument, she threatens to take the kids and leave and he breaks all the way down. I try to give him as much support as possible, but I feel like a therapist. Like I just want to say dam ya'll don't talk. I'm a little stressed out. They have been married awhile and I don't think divorce is an option for him.
_unhappy mistress

My Response

Not your problem, sis.
Noella Fe

I pulled a piece from my mistress mail; I thought it suited this topic. If you blow up every time without giving yourself or your spouse time to assess and grasp the situation then believe me he will seek someone that is going to be patient with him. Don't rush your marriage; don't rush arguments, don't rush sex, don't rush love, don't rush memories. Don't rush kids.

Slow down *sistaladifriend. Now if you are purposely sabotaging your shit then rock out boo. If you feel you have to leave, then leave. The thing about being married is you don't have to leave after an issue but if you do you can go back after an argument. Women in general have emotional responses to just about everything but practice something for me hun, I promise it will not hurt. Throw logics in the game sis. Map it out like a basketball game. Check the offense and the defense positions. See what play needs to be called.

To be honest women run the temperament of the household, no need to have everyone walking on eggshells because you are frustrated. DO NOT INVOLVE THE CHILDREN IN THE DRAMA. For the love of god do not run away with the kids, that shit is traumatizing for everyone involved.

No, talking doesn't solve everything however it allows everyone to be aware and clear of whatever the nature of the issue is. Don't chase your husband away; give yourself time. If you must go to your mama house, remember even then keep your mouth shut. If you can't keep your mouth shut, don't be disloyal to your mate by throwing him under the bus.

The second half of this savory tip is to remember men do a lot of things off of impulse. Sometimes the adrenaline starts booming and the blood rushes to their dick and that is when they make inconsiderate decisions based off of impulse. You have to always be the rational one because in hind-set some actions by men aren't really a thought first. Sorry, you can't respond emotionally to impulsive actions.

For instance, a man will buy an entertainment system when your pregnant instead of diapers and shit. Didn't mean he wasn't thinking of you and the baby and the future, his dick got hard when he saw the 70-inch flat screen and heard the audio, so he purchased it. All he had on the brain at the moment is how he was going too be directly in the ESPN studios or how good *Madden 2k is going to look on this big screen. (shrugs) See very easy for them to get distracted. You don't need a superpower to know that. As a wife though you need to remember this man is trusting you with his vulnerability and all his boyish fantasies. Remember think like a wife not a girlfriend, right?

(You didn't think I was talking about him having sex with another person, did you?) Wifey, another *cooch is not the only thing that excites men, but if you fly off the handle, you'll never get to that point to know most married men aren't thinking about other women. I KNOW, HARD TO BELIEVE, BUT IT'S TRUE DOLL, AND YOU KNOW WHAT? ONCE YOU BELIEVE IT, the universe makes sure of it. I told you, you have magic of your own!

REPEAT AFTER ME; MARRIAGE SHOULD NOT GIVE YOU HIGH BLOOD PRESSURE, LOW BLOOD PRESSURE OR HEAD PRESSURE, NONE OF THAT OK! (SHAKE YOUR HEAD)

If you're having a bad day, take your time. Don't take it out on your mate. It's really about self-control. DON'T HANDLE YOUR HUSBAND LIKE YOU HANDLE EVERYONE ELSE. Even something so simple as when your red light comes on, instead of being bitchy during your period, let him know how much pain your in or get a calendar so he'll know, you would be surprised how loving they can be during this time of the month. Your going to bleed during most of the marriage. Time to simmer down and take time to figure out how these days can be a little easier. You are allowed to be a woman before you should be expected to carry out the role of a wife, HELLO NOT SAYING DON'T BE A DAM WIFE! SOME OF Y'ALL *WENCHES BE CARRYING THINGS TO FAR.

MAIL TIME

Dear Noella,

Ok I read your book, SECRETS OF A HAPPY MISTRESS, even though I am a married woman and one thing that stuck out was when you stated, a lot of married men don't cheat because of sex.

Well I notice that my husband steps out right around that time of the month, like he just finds that he has a lot to do during that week. Granted I am a total bitch when I'm on my period, I don't really want to be bothered, but do you think he could be seeing someone during this time of the month. I MEAN LITERALLY THIS IS THE ONLY TIME HE DISAPPEARS, it's like clockwork.
_on red

My Response
Now lemme me clarify; I am no fortune teller. I can not tell you that your husband isn't cheating; what I will address is this, think positive; he could be just stepping out, not necessarily with another woman. Yes, it's true many men just have a mistress as an extra ear, but have you considered if he is cheating that you are pushing him towards another woman by expressing you don't want to be bothered during your red days? Let him love you up. Nothing better than the attention during your red-light days. I had to pretend to get severe cramps because my period isn't painful, honeeeyyyyyy those hugs are different. SMILE) You are acting like the devil isn't going to slide in and create more chaos in an already intense atmosphere.

I know the pain to be real, but did it occur to you, cause it occurred to me, anger feeds cramps! (throws hands in the air). You are used to going thru your period alone. Its ok, give your husband time to adjust to all the shit that comes with the "monthly." If he loves you, he is paying attention, trying to figure out how to make it better. He isn't a mind reader though speak up. This is your new best friend. YOU ARE HIS WIFE. HUBBY HAS TO "GET WITH THE SHITS." Ok, now a lot of men won't go get the products, that might be pushing it. However, this is not some freak of nature. You admitted that your attitude sucks, so maybe he more than likely gets gone because of that not because your bleeding.

_Noella Fe

ANOTHER thing some of you have to give time to is, the whole sex thing. Yes, by time you get married you should be familiar with all body parts, however sometimes sex isn't the reason people get married, I say a bad sex life can be improved. To be honest this is when if you don't know your body parts that well, now is a perfect start. Shed the clothes baby and let the sensual games married people indulge in begin. Notice I said sensual not sexual, the intimacy has levels as well and as you and your spouse get closer you eat those levels without even realizing it.

A note to women who have gained weight and have a hard time dealing with it, YOU ARE BEAUTIFUL AND IF YOU LOVE YOU FIRST; YOUR HUSBAND WILL LOVE YOU FOR THAT ALONE. I'll touch more on that later.

You have an eternity to fix what you don't like, your husband in a sense is your project, he is yours *sistaladifriend! Don't allow yourself to believe there isn't enough time to make the union better, every day it needs improving and everyday it does improve even when you don't think so.

 I know earlier I gave an example of having babies, but even then, take your time to get to know each other before having children. Believe things do change when you get married. Before you were married, it was girlfriends, best friends, time apart, etc. but not now. It's you and him. That's how it should be. I guarantee if you whisper this secret to yourself and act on it, your husband will either become your best friend, or you will be reassured the reason why this will become your best friend as well as your husband. But even that takes real time so don't rush anything. This is a meal you are preparing, and your marriage is the main course.

 FOR THE ONES THAT READ THE CHAPTER AND STILL DIDN'T SEE THE SECRET (RUSHING YOUR MARRIAGE DOESN'T EQUATE ANYTHING BUT A FAILED MARRIAGE, THE BEST MARRIAGES PUT IN TIME.)

6
THINK LIKE A QUEEN, MOVE LIKE A WIFE
Learn to submit

Ok ok okayyyyy!!

ORDER IN THE DAM COURT!
Before you tear the page out and start going in on me under the Amazon review section hear me out! So many women call themselves queens, and that's fine, but if everyone were a queen then we would have great kingdoms and families would live like clans. Everybody isn't supposed to be a queen. QUEENS SUBMIT IMMEDIATELY AND MOST TIME THEY ARE ASSETS TO THE KING IN WHICH MARRIAGE IS SOUGHT. Understand women through time and even now are groomed from young to marry big. (You know, I like putting you on but just enough so you can explore and read things for yourself.(wink)) In some eastern countries families work hard as hell so they will have a big enough *dowry that will please the Husband in acceptance of this daughter. SHIT REAL, I'm glad to be an American. I think if I had to get married based on a dowry, well I wouldn't be writing books two & three. Whew!
(laughs hard and hysterically.) GIMME A SECOND I ALMOST CHOKED!

Don't make me give examples of queens. For real Hollyhood had ya'll leaving your husbands and being a hot girl all summer, when they themselves were working feverishly on their marriages, being the submissive wife, they knew they always were. There is nothing wrong with submitting to your husband, mind body and soul. HELLO, DON'T LOSE YOURSELF. That is not the message I'm trying to convey to you at all! DON'T EMAIL ME LATER SAYING YOU SUBMITTED NOW YOU SINGLE. BE SUBMISSIVE NOT STUPID.

This is just my chapter to school you on some things that many women don't admit to. I am not talking about a woman that is independent. I'M NOT EVEN ADDRESSING The woman that only got married because her family thought she liked women. THEY will not bother and concern themselves with this section because in reality, most of those women need counseling to get over themselves and the wife role. Truth be told most of those women really never care about their husbands and never conform to the comfort of a man and being married. I have no idea why!

NEVERTHELESS, this section addresses the wife that directly wants to a wife, not just another married woman. There are wives who don't appreciate want or care about their husbands or a man for that matter. Not because they are gay or whatever but because they just built ford tough.

NOT THE KID BABY... Don't get me wrong I've always had some *blackness about myself but I am one hundred percent woman, and my husband let me be as such.

Back to what I was saying. In this chapter I didn't have any mail to attach to this chapter because not a lot of women want to have THIS type of conversation. We are in the day and age where the conversation is still women need to take control. Or be head of household I'll cover that later.

Many things separate a woman from a queen. And even more differences that separate a queen from a wife. (breathe) Yup I said it. If you were not aware of that pay attention. All great queens that ruled had to pardon a lot of things as a queen that would destroy the ordinary wife. Get over yourself! If you think your going through a lot as just a wife, I'm going to need you to start reading more or looking up Queens of past. My stepmother always said it's only one queen to a castle. Now I know why she never referred to herself as a wife, she put up with a lot of shit. (You'll have to wait on that book to find out what she went thru.)

I'm not saying you're not a queen. I'm asking you to think how your sacrifice game is setup. Sacrifice has nothing to do with compromise and queens don't really comprise they sacrifice, and that is far greater than compromising. I hear so many women scream about the fifty-fifty bull crap, they be fake happy. Remember the mail from chapter two right, the laundry lady? If not go back, great example of how fifty/fifty works. (looks sideways, burst into laughter) If you married a man on the premises of 50/50, it's going to take a lot more than these secrets to get to your happy wife's place.

Your vocabulary can also affect your harmony. The logic behind half to me means that you are only giving me half. What in the hell does meet me halfway mean? In my little head my first question is, who got to the halfway point first? Second, is one of us waiting on the other person? Third, is there a rule on the pace of things in this kind of set up? You see where I'm going with this? So, when you say half you only asking for half of woman or man in my opinion. (shakes head with lip curled up) *nawwww, I don't think so. (shakes head from side to side)

I want 100% man. Your spouse is supposed to make you a better woman, you should already be a hell of a woman and you should not put up with someone that falls short either. If you're broken, get you somebody broken so you can build each other back up. Stop marrying below your level. May sound harsh, but it's a sure way to destruction. That is also one way you separate the QUEENS FROM THE WIVES, queens don't struggle love or marry *questionable-potential. (Shrugs) It is what it is, and I said what I said, and I will not retract this statement.

Queens always bring just what the king needs. What do you have that can be multiplied? What connects can you and your family benefit from? What connections do you have for your husband? What's your asset? HEAR ME CLEARLY! I'm NOT SUGGESTING YOU RAISE A MAN; there is no way possible you can submit to a boy. That's not a queen nor a wife that's called playing the mother.
......

Oh, really quick, Queens know having babies is a big part of her crown. Them bitches rather die by the sword than not produce an heir. Your favorite R&B singer thought she was going keep her body and have kids when she was ready but had you drinking lemonade. (shrugs) She learned the hard way that she was never to be just a wife. I'm telling you being a wife ain't bad. Husbands love, Kings Rule. You determine the position you wanna play, but dammit you better do it right which ever you decide. Back to the gem.

It's easier to be a wife, but I like the challenge of maintaining my queendom. I'm just telling you to have the mindset of a queen. Pick your poison. Don't take off more than you can chew. This goes double if you're married to an athlete or anyone with a high paying stressful job; you can wear your crown rightfully. It takes a powerful woman to endure what a lot of high-profile trophy wives go thru. Sure, they have a fairytale, but what fairytales have you ever seen that didn't involve someone having a nightmare? You can also save yourself a lot of heartaches if you ask yourself simple questions like I am asking you now. These chapters are a little intense, but... lighten up doll; it's only the rest of your life we are possibly discussing.

Many, many things can come in left field in your marriage, including other women. Sometimes a mistress is called into play by the wife. Now this is where the queen would differ from the wife. I am not telling you to have threesomes, orgies etc but I am telling you to decide the lane you and your marriage is in and stick to it. You are the power behind this union. Run your ship the way you want. Say no when you're not comfortable. Please don't wait ten years to say, no more swinger clubs!!!! You don't have to be a queen; the wife is good enough for your husband.

TO THE GROUP OF PEOPLE LOOKING FOR THEIR CROWNS, IN CASED YOU MISSED SECRET NUMBER SIX! EVERY QUEEN IS A WIFE, BUT EVERY WIFE DOESN'T HAVE TO BE A QUEEN, JUST THINK LIKE ONE.

7
KEEP IT CLASSY, STAY NASTY AND AVOID BEING TRASHY
You's married now! Time to open up!

My favorite chapter! I had the most fun writing this one. Now the book is coming from one wife to another, however this section is also talking to the hoe in you ok. I said wife comes with many titles, this is one. All women have an inner hoe, and she has had to replace us mentally on several occasions. AIN'T NOTHING WRONG IF, "*HOE IS LIFE" was *a wave at one point in your life until you met your Prince Charming. Now I'ma keep it all the way real with you ladies in this chapter. Get your wine if you don't have a drop of freak in your genes. This chapter might be beyond intense for you. From one hoe– I mean, wife! From one wife to another; You have to be ready for this married sex life, baby!

LADIES NOW I'M NOT GOING TO BULLSHIT YOU BABYYYYYYY; this Is where I had to make some tough decisions. I couldn't keep it nasty lololololol. Now I still kept it freaky for my husband. I just couldn't keep up with *sucking him off after like six years! LIKE DAMN! I'm surprised I never caught lockjaw! (Blinks eyelashes fast) Unless you're going to do what I did I need you to suck all this info in and remember what I am telling you like you remember your mom's birthday. AS A MATTER OF FACT DON'T SUCK IT ALL IN. SAVE YOUR SALIVA FOR YUR HUSBAND(LOLOLOLOLOL) just keep real good mental notes.

MAIL TIME

DEAR NOELLA FE,

Ok so I've been married for about three years and I think my husband thinks I'm a porn star. I don't mind the freaky shit but the other night he kinda made gestures towards him wanting me to go past his penis. I was kinda shocked. ESPECIALLY because he is so masculine. I tried to honor his request, but I was literally sick and I changed my mind. It was way beyond awkward. I'M LOST ON THIS ONE.
_Not a real freak

(Looks over glasses)

My Response

*Honey, I didn't let the snake bite my tongue! Chile, WHAT? (rolls eyes) YOU WANNA KNOW WHAT I DID? I could not keep sucking my husbands dick! No way! I tapped out and allowed my husband to go outside of our marriage for his sexual needs. (Shrugs) YES! (claps) I! (claps) DID! (claps)!

I was not willing to perform. *Bihhhhh I got *muthafkin-tied. I'm not saying for you to do that, but you first need to think about what you are willing to do or not do then talk about it. It sounds like your husbands been holding back if your stunned by the request to east his ass, and to be honest he may not have wanted you to go that far. There is a spot in between the balls and ass that when is touched in the correct way, makes a man holler(shrugs) I don't think you should approach it with shame nor guilt, it's nothing but a conversation, sounds like you guys need to open up in your marriage on both parts, Look for book 3! Secrets of a Happy Marriage(wink)
_Noella Fe

NOW FOCUS ON WHAT I'M SUGGESTING YOU DO.

Never believe that sex is supposed to end or that "it" gets boring after a while. If that's the case, you might be the boring one (shrugs). Another hat you will wear as a wife is the creative director. Get your theater skills up. Now you can always take the easy way out and get a new cooch if you feel it's keeping you and hubby from hot steamy, passionate love. Jada Pickett did. She said, "She has the veejay of a 16-year-old!" (grabs imaginary pearls) Dam shame then the bitch turned around and said SHE STILL WASN'T HAPPY UNTIL 2019 (sips). So, don't run out and nip and tuck your twat; it still doesn't make you happy.

If you don't have *stacks-on-racks like old girl, now is an excellent time to find yourself. Get in tune with yourself sexually so you and hubby can have explosive sex. Do you know I once met a woman who at the ripe age of 45 had never stuck her finger in her twat? (falls out) Sayyyy whatttt? Right, I don't know what tribe these hoes came from. If this is you, that means you ain't never really fucked nobody! Maybe. (Tilts head) Sounds like you had a privileged life of just *laying on your back.* Sorry to break the news to you, but if you have only had 'on your back sex,' you're a *bed-wench, not a wife. On top of that's girlfriend behavior. Your hubby might step out on you for someone that has substance. (shrugs) (blinks and sip)

It's also possible the men you had sex with before hubby just didn't want to hurt your feelings. Or it could be a 'hoe was life' situation, I GET IT!

Ok, ok Lucky you. You found someone to love you and the fact that you just lay there like a lump on a log. LISTEN THIS IS A GOOD REASON FOR HIM TO LEAVE YO ASS or get a mistress but like I was saying you found someone to love you, and he is not a complainer, for the love of god do something different. I promise you will enjoy it just as much as him; it will be like a whole new sex partner.
Sex is a large genre. It's not only about penetration. There are plenty of things you can do if the organs ain't/don't/won't work properly. Once again, TAKE YOUR TIME. You might have to coach hubby. If he fucks like a jack rabbit, it's ok now you have time to work on it. If you had a good life *laying on your back* as I stated, time to do something different or new. Trust me, sweetheart, your husband, is expecting you to become a porn star.

Men are just as sexual as women. When you are having good, free, sex that's mixed with intense passion and love, sorry but there are no boundaries. If there are boundaries set up for your sex life, more than likely you crossed those boundaries to know that there is one. When you are warmed up, you're not thinking or rather you shouldn't be thinking about what society deems morally correct in your bedroom. Many men hope that at some point they can be open about certain preferences or curiosities.

THIS IS ONE OF THOSE THINGS YOU KEEP TO YOURSELF. IF YOU'RE LICKING YOUR MAN ASS, the only way it's going to get out if you act like a girlfriend instead of a wife and open up your mouth and tell someone. Girlfriends act childish when it comes to real grown-up sex. He is not going to tell anyone that he likes for you to blow his hole. Maybe he will I don't know, lol. Be a leader not a follower. If he is telling secrets tell him this, "While you running your mouth about what I do to you, guaranteed your 'man' is thinking about me doing it to him or watching me do it." Then smile. HI FIVE! (Queen Move, chapter 5.) The same ones who laugh with you and your man will be the same ones that judge your filthy confessions. Your good girlfriend is going tell all her other friends and all the men she is laying with because she's a child too.

Of course, you shouldn't be made out to be a porn star, but it would help if you would volunteer to be one.

Don't get this chapter or any page in this book confused with some janky advice on how to keep your husband. Only god can hold him, not sex, not a meal, not shit. The goal of this book is to open you up to keeping your life as simple, cute and stress free as possible. (Smile, I'm on your side)

Let me say this to you, if you can pop your ass or twerk in public at any point you shouldn't be scared of your man, like for real. Marriage doesn't mean boring sex or the freak in you must be put away, you just need to reserve shit like that for your man. You be you in the end but all I'm saying is there is a group of women that exist, that live life just to twerk, pop ass and be as slutty as possible in public arenas, including the internet but will cry about getting a finger stuck in they ass during sex WITH THIER HUSBAND.

Ok you just a nasty freak, can't control it and he still married you. GOOD! However, let me throw another *battery in your back*. (twist lip) While you out here showing out, your husband is looking for a shy freak on the side that he might can whisk away with a couple of close friends. *IJS, never do anything outside your house that you wouldn't do inside the house and never do the shit you do indoors, outside. Oh, and never tell hubby how trashy your friends are either, some shit stays between friends. Don't think by telling your man that your friends are sluts are going to make him think of them in a negative light on the flip side, the only thing it will do is give him ideas on what you should be doing to him. If you're not a freak like I said, somethings you're going to either have to let go of, or add to. Pick your poison. Just don't make any irrational decisions without talking to hubby first. Again, don't do anything you're not comfortable with, and if your husband can't understand that, then now is the time to think if this is the husband for you. TO THE PEOPLE COMPLAINING ABOUT LICKING THE G-SPOT, JUST IN CASE YOU MISSED SECRET NUMBER SEVEN, BE A PORN STAR IN BED AND A WIFE IN PUBLIC.

8
BEFORE YOU QUIT, BEFORE YOU HAND DOWN SENTENCING
Solve the Crime That Has Been Committed

You have to be the judge, the jury, and be ready to bear the burden of proof when it comes to addressing issues within your marriage, whether it's physical or not. Especially crimes of infidelity. Do not trust other sources on matters of such, not even your mama, if you scared or concerned don't go to church, go to a private investigator. IJS too many marriages end off of false information.

Women are natural born private investigators. However, when something happens such as infidelity some of us fail to investigate the whole situation. We only gather the evidence that coincides with the thought of the man being guilty. You have everyone that has a solution, but yet you yourself don't really know the damn problem. I know, I know; A woman's intuition is always right. I also know sometimes we fail to pay attention to it until things blow up in our face, we miss the signs. NO, WE IGNORE THE SIGNS. THUS, WE CHEAT OURSELVES WAY BEFORE OUR HUSBANDS EVER HAD A CHANCE TO.

MAIL TIME

Dear Noella,

I follow you on Facebook, and you were on a show and you mentioned that there is no such thing as cheating. I disagree. How can you say that when men and women cheat every day? I think you and most of your views are way off. There is no way you can advocate that, it's facts. I'm in my 50's and I have been cheated on multiple times
Your delusional
thinks nothing of your words

My Response

Simple, I say this because you and most women ignore feelings, ignoring your body is/was where you fucked up. It doesn't matter what anybody tells you, you have common sense hopefully and hopefully you will use it in the future being you have been cheated on before. That alone should put you the predicament NOT to be cheated on again. I can advocate "I haven't been cheated on" because myself and a host of women can testify to never being cheated on.

If you know your partner like you say you do, like most women claim too, then you will know when your partner is inching another way. Know your man. I promote what to do before it gets to someone stepping out. If you scared to tell your man, someone else turned you on or vice verse, then that might not be the person for you. I don't deal with adults that lie, that's what children do. I also said in my book, SECRETS OF A HAPPY MISTRESS, more wives knowest than not, meaning women know their husbands are stepping out. ONCE YOU KNOW, IT AIN'T CHEATING NO MORE. You may be dealing with a liar but a cheater they are not.
_Noella Fe

You're supposed to gain more superpowers being a wife. In no way are you supposed to have a union with someone and not gain on top of losing yourself. Your woman power is not supposed to decrease in anyway. It was you that decided not to say anything once your "intuition" kicked in. Your intuition will have nothing on facts. You can only get that two ways by mouth or observation. Now if your hubby switches up on you, don't wait to ask what you are already thinking.

Now, this little bitty chapter talks to the wife that for whatever reason assumes her forever is cheating. I didn't think you all needed to much mail for this chapter especially because when it comes to this topic, every situation is different. I wanted to directly address you and this journey you are on. Really this chapter is about how to address the situation before it leads to infidelity.

Some of y'all are rabbit ass crazy! You're possessive, carrying around trauma from your mother being a serial cheater. YUP some of y'all mamas is off the chain and you grew up seeing that shit all your life. If this is the case, you have got to get professional help to deal with this. I know too many men that have lost whole hairlines! I mean young men too! Stressed all the way out because its routine for their wife to wake up mad as hell due to a dream she had of him cheating and to her that was a sign. (slaps forehead)

Don't get me wrong, sometimes it is a sign of something, All I'm saying is gather facts after a vision. You don't think it's silly to go off a vision you only see when your eyes are closed? Let me know so I can make it a topic in the upcoming panel I'll be holding in 2020, "Marriage, Men & Mistresses."

As the jury, you have to examine everything. Hold all parties involved accountable for the information you receive. This is not some high school 'he said she said' game. "Don't tell your husband I said this", is the deadliest sentence a person can say to you when condemning your husband or accusing him of going against you are stepping out on you. This includes co-workers, homeboys, family members and if a woman is involved then her too. I like to gather every little piece of information. I am not going off of any half ass misinformation. I'm more worried about the mindset behind the action than the actual crime itself and to obtain that information it takes a little more skill than the average wife is willing to apply. You saw how Hillary Clinton did our president! Threw his ass right to the wolves when the Monica Lewinsky scandal broke. I DON'T CARE she shouldn't have done Uncle Bill like that. She was no longer my First Lady after that. She was a typical woman. Bitch was going let it all go over a fuckin dress & an intern? OKAYYYYYY, if you that type of wife, I feel really bad for your husband. I SAID WHAT I SAID. Most women are really quick to to jump on the side of the person pointing the finger. This is another area where you need to take your time. Baby, ain't nothing worse than accusing your husband publicly, only to retract your shit to the same audience. For real this has nothing to do with your husband, It's about you and your reaction. Holding him down thru something as egregious as having an affair, shows your strength and character that will always be seen and

remembered. QUEEN SHIT.

Don't just let anyone come and tell you something about your marriage or husband without you fully investigating. Look at all the thirst buckets that came out claiming to be pregnant by somebody husband to find out she was lying the whole time. The crazy part is the wife has gone on social media posting subs about no good men, then blasting their man, all in twenty-four hours based on the feelings of the Instagram Crime Unit.

On another note don't take people close to you for granted either. Meaning just cause y'all tighter than glue since the fifth grade don't mean they won't *shoot a shot*. Things become inferno-like because information was given to you from a trusted source. Understandable that your first thought is this person wouldn't lie to me. I do not care that it came from a longtime homeboy of his. Those ones and his uncles are trying to fuck on the low especially if he is disclosing what that mouth do behind closed doors. Just as some women say they gotta watch their friends, you gotta watch his friends too. Hell, what you think to be a moment of *hoe'ism* on your husband's part, might be an inside job all along because the homie either want you or want him.(shrugs) Is there another reason for a man to be jealous of the wife of his best friend? Listen to me very carefully, it's not always another woman interfering in your martial affairs.

Have you ever heard of family members plotting
and setting up scenarios for the ex to "bump" into
your husband? Hmmmmm, Just because everyone
was at the reception does not mean they was
rooting for y'all at the chapel. (sips) Most men
brush off things women deem strange.
I know somebody need an example; here you go:
Your husband's happy ass isn't even thinking
anything about another woman; especially any
woman before you. Thus, the reason he didn't tell
you he ran into his ex GIRLFRIEND at the mall. His
silly ass didn't even think it was strange that both
her sons came to the gym you were at, claiming
they thought their mom was here with their aunt. All
along the dam mama-in-law done set the shit up!
(Throws hands to the heavens) I'm just giving
examples for the people in the back that need me to
dumb it down a little. I actually have women that
have been through this kind of madness. Hell, I
think I've been a victim of this crime, I just can't put
my finger on it. Communication prevented shit from
going left in my situation.

Some family members are just disrespectful! You remember "Player's Club", where the cousin was sleeping with the other cousin's husband while she out stripping? Take that scenario and learn from it. No one can be trusted with your man, that's not something you should be worried about. Your husband is who you are married to only he owes you trust, loyalty and honesty. Have faith in god that he sent you a man made of all those things. Now this isn't a Christian book but let me throw this in there.

DON'T LEAN ON GOD WHEN YOU CHOOSE TO REMAIN A FOOL. What do I mean by this statement? Women go thru hell and swear they are waiting on god to give them an answer. Many miss the dam message he be sending directly to you. Instead, you go to your pastor he tells you to stay, your family members tell you to stay, yet god has already filled your heart with the spirit of flight. You can't sleep, YOUR MIND WANDERS, sex is different, GIRL, GOD IS TRYING TELL YOU SOMETHING! (IN MY SHUG AVERY VOICE) (THE LADY IN THE MOVIE," THE COLOR PURPLE" FOR NON-BLACK FOLK & PEOPLE WHO ONLY WATCH SHIT ON IG, & YOUTUBE) LIKE I SAID IN THE OTHER CHAPTER, BE SUBMISSIVE, NOT STUPID.

This is the main reason you must allow free communication once you are married. It is you that will set the tone in how free you two will flow. Make your man comfortable with coming to tell you anything & everything. BITCH! YOU BETTER LISTEN TO PRINCE, he was the lover, the brother, the friend, the mother and the earth all in one! You my dear have to gather yourself and be ready to receive these types of conversation. Do not shrug off your feelings if they are real and not coming from a place of insecurity, and don't dismiss your husband's words or concerns.

I had to many letters about infidelity and how to handle it, most of the letters or emails were pertaining to assumptions, only a few had clear facts. In the cases of those women and men that were really going thru a rough patch and couldn't tell but had a notch that their spouse was seeing someone else; my solid advice was hire a private investigator. The movie, 'She Devil' with Roseanne Barr was the funniest but realest movie out about how this woman found out her husband was having an affair. I think it came out in the 80's not sure but what I am for sure about is, this movie showed one classy way to go about being a happy wife even in the darkest of times.

Invest in your dam marriage. I am strictly against involving outsiders (besides those involved) in tangled webs. Plus, if you decide to stick it out, that's you and your husband's business. Judgement is for god not man. Some men love women and some of you know that, don't make your guy the bad guy when you knew from the start. If your business gets out, stand tall and beside your man. All I'm suggesting to you is, check everything out. I like to gather and question in stages and I only reveal the source or seasoning if necessary. Another thing you have to think about is how you handle the crime if one has been committed. If you're going to forgive, remember darling heal first then forgive if that's what you decide to do. It will not be an easy road if you lie to yourself and forgive when you can't. Do not believe anyone that tells you to put up with being a number instead of a wife.

One more thing. Do not charge one with an offense if you are also committing or have committed an offense. Some of y'all are out here terrorizing your damn husbands and you are messy as hell. Your girlfriends might not tell you this and your mama might not either especially if she was *hoeing but girl, nothing is worse than a man that has been accused and his wife is the one cheating. Be humble *sis. Karma comes quick. (tilts head)

FOR THE PEOPLE TOO BUSY DENYING WOMEN
HAVE AFFAIRS, SECRET NUMBER EIGHT, AFTER
AND INJUSTICE HAS BEEN DONE TO YOU AND
YOUR UNION, GATHER ALL INFO FIRST, HOLD
PEOPLE ACCOUNTABLE THEN TAKE ACTION. IF
YOU DECIDE TO STAY IN YOUR UNION, YOU
DON'T HAVE TO FORGET, JUST FORGIVE &
MOVE FORWARD.

I would have died versus stripping my husband of his manhood. I was completely devoted to protecting it without ever being physical or verbal. -Noella Fe

9

YOU CAN WEAR PANTS BUT LET YOUR HUSBAND BE THE MAN

I know I said my favorite chapter was what I said it was
(I love them all) but I really like this chapter; this is all I see all over the damn internet from a lot of single women that feel they will run over their husband. I see just as many that are married posting nonsense about how they pay the bills and they are the bread winner. FINE! THERE IS NOTHING WRONG WITH HAVING A, "MR.MOM". IF YOU DON'T KNOW WHAT THAT IS WATCH THE MOVIE. *(cheese)

There is an epidemic that is going on. The women of the 20th century want to be the man and the woman in the relationship. This is why I disagree with the whole 50/50 thing. Its stupid to me for this very reason. My husband did not want to switch roles and when it came a time where my paper held more weight, that was our secret. I never carried it over my husband, and I damn sure didn't let anyone know. When we stepped out in the public's eye, he was the husband and I his wife, in the house I was a woman and he the man of the house. That never changed.

This has nothing to do with if you make more money, it has nothing to do with your status and how your man appears to the outside world. This chapter is how you present yourself in public with your husband and how people view both of you.

MAIL TIME

Dear Noella,

A couple of weeks ago my brother told me I was out of line because of the way I talk to my husband. I don't see anything wrong with the way I talk to him. I'm an alpha female and I'm dominant. My brother is not even married. I came across your YouTube and I thought I would hit you up because you seem to think you know everything about marriage and cheating. I mean my husband doesn't say anything. After he cheated like he can't say much anyway, I decided to take him back and now it is what it is. I'm not sure what you promote, but you are suggesting that I be docile while my husband runs a muck is not helping real situations.
_I am a boss

(sips jack)

My Response

YOU SHOULD NEVER WANT TO TAKE YOUR HUSBANDS MANHOOD even if he steps out on you. Yup, I said it. DEAL WITH THAT SHIT, you think you a boss because you're dominating your husband? GURL I HAVE TIME TAHDAY! That's stupid. Especially if you weren't the dominant one beforehand. Nothing wrong with taking control of things but you have a man telling you how it looks to another man, you might want to consider what your husband and you look like as a couple. Remember you are your husband at the end of the day and it's you and him. If he looks bad, sorry sis, you look extra bad. I promote a healthy living, if you forgive you need to move forward and if you can't, move on. If you have kids, your teaching your kids some wicked, weak lessons that will leave them scorned, hurt and delusional. Kudos to you for that too!
_Noella Fe

Side Bar: Seriously, you have an issue and need to seek help if you feel that you are in control, after you let your husband come back to you after infidelity just to make him suffer. You are a control freak, maybe even timid or cowardly; and now you are a bully. Pain don't help pain sweetness.
WAIT! STOP! BEFORE YOU GET ALL ITCHY IN THE ASS!
I said, 'deal with it'. I did not tell you how to do so, and I would never. I will say, control your energy.

Look at you!
Ready to get *twitter-fingers on me, I know
someone read that last paragraph and was like hold
up no the f--- she didn't. You're right I didn't.
*lmao

MAIL TIME

Dear Noella Fe Says,
Hey, I think your pretty dope for a female, you talk
like how a man think but you stay a woman, lol. So
basically, I'm married, and my wife is extra saucy, it
don't bother me all the time but I was thinking she
would simmer down a bit, She talks reckless but I
don't think she should talk reckless to me. I told her
on some play shit, but now that things are over the
top for even me, I'm not sure how to address it. I
don't wanna lose my wife, but I don't want to
compromise my manhood either.
_Man Rant

My Response

Your wife, your life buddy! You knew what and who
you married. My advice to anyone that can't
verbally express themselves, put it on paper. I can't
tell you to put up with anything that decreases your
self esteem. What I will say is this; As you said, 'I
speak like a man.'

Lol, if you thought that, know I pipe down when I'm with my husband. I'm definitely not confrontational with him and nor he to I. We just didn't do that to each other. There is a difference between being spicy versus mean. *WTF wants to deal with a manly woman, hi five to you. Communication is key if nothing else try therapy to get to the root of why she feels like she has to be like this. Good Luck Hun!

_Noella Fe

Side Bar: Men be short and to the point. I feel bad, I have seen women like that, and it turns my stomach. I really wanted to tell him to run. Those bitches are scary. If you are a man reading this book and 'Man Rant' just described your scenario, your wife has some trauma she hasn't dealt with. Those women need extra love and for real the men who deal with women like that, let alone marry them, are actually the strongest of men to me heart wise. To deal with a bossy, loud, controlling female is beyond the men I know.

This, my friend I can assure you if you stay in the lane as a wife you will be happier than the wife that tries to be her husband. That shit is about control you never had over your own life. Marriage nor any other title gives anyone the right to try and control another human being. It never amazes me when women complain about the load they carry in their arrangement when in fact they want to do everything. HUH? For that you could have stayed single. WE TALKED ABOUT THAT REMEMBER? STOP THINKING SINGLE AND START ACTING MARRIED.

Now when it comes to house duties, I can truly say I was blessed with a husband that could do everything for himself. I love that my husband can cook and even better that it was no issue for him to cook. Because I wasn't bogged down with the weight of the world, I had time to cook, so he didn't have to. Another thing that I find that goes with this chapter is, when arguing don't downgrade or degrade him, don't argue in public either. Many women take advantage of public places. Normal men don't react and allow you to act like a complete fool around other people. Why do we do that? Simply because we are women; out of control at times and very extra. No other reason why you would flip tables, call his mama a bitch, throw water on him, and still expect to ride home with that man.

We test and tempt our husbands and then cry wolf when he takes the bait. Don't mess up the natural order of things by testing him. As a wife you don't have to test anything. You should have done all the testing before you signed that piece of paper. Stop setting traps.

To all my alpha dominant wives, unless you know your man can't fight, don't get involved in man things. Don't take it upon yourself to react over something he either A) he told you, B) you found out or C) you heard.

I know the people in the back need an example so here you go,

Example: Your husband tells you his brother is cheating, you run off and tell his wife because y'all cool and you even have the nerve to call your brother in law and give him more than your two cents, you give him every cent in your child's piggy bank.

(PAUSEEE, SLOWWWW DOWN) First let your man police his brother. It doesn't matter that he might not say it like you, or he might be indirect, shut up! For the real hard-headed ones do not go against your husband if he tells you to leave something alone. You make him look stupid.

Another thing that kept me happy, I did not associate with his friends. Some of y'all are very sneaky, building this bond with your husband's friends. You borrow money, you confide in them, you even console them. NOPE, NOT SUPPOSE TO HAPPEN. I don't care that everybody went to college together; only two of you got married. If you are going to discuss your issues and problems your husband should be present, and don't even try the whole "you want to know how to be a better wife" thing. Ask your damn husband.

Things can go left and get messy quick! Just don't do it. I already told you don't talk about your man to other people, that's a straight weapon against your husband. Another thing that irks the hell out of me is, wives putting their husbands in really bad positions because you have a big mouth, If you are out with your man or even without him don't put him in a position where him or you could get hurt because you wanna talk shit on the strength you have a husband to protect you. DO NOT EVER PICK FIGHTS WITH OTHER MEN and put your husband in danger especially if you know he can't fight. Take your macho ass home and drag your non confrontational man home with you. (laughs out loud) On the other hand, if you married a jalapeño pepper don't get into some permanent shit you will regret forever. Like getting your husband locked up or even worse killed. Please don't be one of those women that pick, provoke and then run to your husband crying wolf. There will always be someone bigger, badder, meaner, tougher than you and your husband. Nobody wants to be a widow especially by their own hand.

TO THE PEOPLE IN THE BACK A LITTLE CONFUSED, SECRET NUMBER NINE, DON'T OVERRULE OR UNDERESTIMATE YOUR HUSBAND. Men only have pants to wear, trousers are optional for women.

10
WIFE IS JUST A TITLE AND CAN BE REMOVED
You will always be you regardless of a title

This chapter is a serious one and most important thus the reason why it is the last chapter. There is nothing wrong with working on your marriage, but I will not do what every other professional has done and tell you to stay when you are no longer overjoyed about being a wife. Listen carefully, not when it is no longer beneficial to you, but when your marriage has no joy and your daily wife life is past overbearing. It's more than ok to consider a new life.

MAIL TIME

Dear Noella,

As you know I'm going thru a divorce right now. First thank you for all your encouragement along the way. I know you get tired of me, but today is one of those days, I cannot grasp that I am going to be out in this world single. He seems happy about separating, and I am just stuck. I was on his fb page again; which I think he is keeping public so that I can see it. He has just closed this chapter. I am not sure if I am venting or need that extra raw advice, I so need to hear.
_not ready to be single

(This letter is from one of my ongoing clients, who in fact had a good amount of feedback for this mini book, I appreciate her and thank her for allowing me to put her personal business in this book.)

My Response

I cannot stress this enough, think hard before you want a divorce. At this point it's you not him. There are men willing to stay married even if not for their own happiness and you my dear weren't happy and he wasn't that type of husband. TAKE THAT HOW YOU FEEL IT (lol). You have what's called separation anxiety and to be honest don't push yourself to start over immediately. The length of your marriage wasn't a five- or ten-year thing. Listen, being a wife is not easy, one day at a time. Be happy with your decision to part ways, even if that is all you know. It's extra important you don't lose yourself, just in case it ends. If you know you were 100% wife, walk away with your head up. Don't let your fear of being single play on your emotions.
_NoellaFe

The real reason I was confident as a wife is because I chose to be one! Even though it is supposed to be forever till death do part; I wasn't waiting till death if I wasn't happy. Never did I pressure myself to live up to this whole wife thing. Don't get me wrong I was a wife all the way, but I was just being me. Everything I did I wanted to. I never regretted being married to the person I was married to. I was a happy wife until I didn't want to be a wife anymore, my joy was never compromised and guess what, me not wanting to be a wife had nothing to do with unhappiness. It had more to do with realizing I didn't want the responsibility of a business marriage anymore. I didn't walk down the aisle for love. The love that my husband and I formed did not result in marriage, it resulted in a friendship. I'm not the only wife that is happy. I'm just apart of the few that didn't have to go through tragedy, or a round two, to know I was a happy wife. A lot of books that came out between 2016 and 2018 were about women who found a new independence, after a bitter divorce. Advice came from women who had to find themselves. I'm not knocking anyone's journey, A good male friend said to me, "For a person to tell someone to be happy they had to know unhappiness first". I understand where he was coming from, but I don't live by those standards. Heartbreak is promoted first, then the victory. Women only want to win after they have been knocked down. I get it. Sometimes the only way people understand things is because they went through whatever. Hey, however, you find the

motivation even if it's through misery, then *do you. The best part is being inspired. Hopefully, my book will save women and men somewhere so that it won't be another sad love song.

It's ok if you throw the towel in especially after effort has been applied. Sometimes you find that being a wife is just not for you, be honest hun. Bitter divorces stem from unhappy wives. I haven't gotten a divorce yet but if you're reading this it's the same formula almost. Marriage can go wrong for many other reasons besides infidelity. If it goes wrong don't blame yourself. While in the marriage don't deprive yourself; make sure your needs are being fulfilled. It's hard running a castle, your crown may tilt, you may even remove it but baby, it will never fall off as long as you secure it. Remember think like a queen act like a wife, right. A queen doesn't lose the crown because a king no longer chooses her. Her crown was already secured before him he was just supposed to strengthen it.

Listen chile, there are plenty of men out there. Who says there is a cap on how many times you can get married? Look at Elizabeth Taylor! Did you know the reason she was married so many times was because her rule was to sleep with her, you had to marry the coochie! (Falls out dies and comes back to life) ···

If that isn't gangsta! Shit, it's a respectable way to keep boyfriends away and open invitations for husband material. (wink) If you can understand that. The main thing that you keep in mind is this isn't supposed to be rough, unkind or unfair. Titles mean nothing if the soul is being compromised in an ungodly way.

Marriage is a luxury not a must, it does not define a woman. Every woman is different and unique, and it has nothing to do with what is in between your legs and everything to do with what's between your ears.

YOU'RE A WHOLE WIFE NOW, no need to worry about the bag; you secured that with your wedding vows! I DARE YOU, go for the crown gorgeous! FOR THE PEOPLE THAT SPED READ TO THE LAST CHAPTER AND ZOOMED PASSED SECRET NUMBER TEN, HERE IT IS IN PLAIN ENGLISH, YOU ARE A HUMAN BEING FIRST, A WOMAN NEXT, BEING A WIFE IS OPTIONAL. In the end you will be a woman still, it's up to you the type of woman you become after a divorce.

See you in Book Three!

Letters to all the different readers

To the soon to be wife:

I wanted to write a book that wasn't long and full of
big words. Everybody has advice and some of it you
don't need. But if you're feeling all scary and
butterflies are churning your stomach; DON'T TRY,
just get the head right and capture each butterfly
and release it. Talk to your fiancé and open up
about the past. Live in the present and dispel any
future fears. Communicate, Communicate,
Communicate!! It is a beautiful thing, waking up
every day to the person that vowed to love, protect,
and honor you. Do Noella a small favor, make sure
in your heart this is what you want to do. Marriage
is meant to be forever; remember it's more than
sex. Don't waste time on trying to be the wife who
doesn't get cheated on either. It's time to stop
speculating like a girlfriend and planning as a wife.
(wink) Congratsssssssssss!

To the right now wife:

The good *lort I serve (starts praise dancing) Sorry,
As I was saying, God knows I am not telling you
how to run your marriage but if you are not happy
what do you have to lose. Try this before you take
notes from a single person or some broad who is
only writing her book because she had a bad
experience and truth be told; Ms. Lady is still bitter
as hell. Hi five girlfriend you have made it this far.
This life is something different. Enjoy and celebrate
yourself as an individual and a wife. There will be a
fair share of bad days but get closer to your man,
learn him and most importantly, let that man learn
you. Just as anything else, this thang got levels
baby!!! Get you some knee pads, and a helmet cause
these men, my god! Things get rough! But
sometimes rough doesn't mean not fun. Number one
piece of advice: You can't make anybody wanna be
with you! Take into consideration when you know in
your heart, it's time to move on. GROW UP! Think
like a queen, move as a wife.

To the wife about to be divorced:

Life isn't over if you lived well. Fill your heart with all the good things and take all the negative and throw it away, minus the lessons that may have come with the bad times. You will continue to live well. If you didn't do anything but live and die for your marriage, IT'S TIME FOR YOU TO START LIVING YOUR BEST LIFE! You didn't go thru a divorce to be unhappy. Even if it was under harsh circumstances let it go, take your time and don't jump right back into a relationship. Baby, you got the golden touch, once a wife always wife material. Don't expect the next marriage to be like the last. So many women make the mistake of trying to get back to what they are used to. Let that life go. It isn't a downgrade, experience new things. Plus, it is not fair for you to hold the new husband accountable for what the old husband used to do. As a fact, keep the memories but get excited about the future ones you haven't created yet. DO NOT LET ANY MAN AFTER YOUR HUSBAND TREAT YOU LESS THAN YOUR HUSBAND DID. Please don't be the wife that goes in circles. When you know better do better. Much luck doll!!

To the normal reader that just thought my book cover was classy and clean!

If your new or a regular, thank you for your support! Thank you for taking your precious time to read my thoughts! If you have time stop by the website, sistaladifriend.com or Amazon and leave a review. That would really make my eyes light up. I'm still a new author your advice and comments are everything to me. Book Three will be out in 2020. God bless all of you

FE'ISM
(Glossary)

I heard you loud and clear with the first book and understand some of my jargon got the better of the message I was trying to send. To make it easier and lessen the emails from the editorial intellects, I added my meanings of some of the terminology, gestures and or sayings. This isn't a scholarly piece so I'm not following the normal format. The glossary goes by page to make it easier for some readers. Plus I was drinking wine and kept forgetting the order of my ABC's. (Blinks really fast) 5xs (giggles)

*original lingo/slang/phrase/gesture made up by author.
**Lingo/slang/phrase/gesture already in public use.

Page 3
**Queer – Strange or Odd.
Page 4
*Mista– A pet name for Husband.
*Talk my Talk– Ability pop junk in a skillful way.
*Deep-Throat Wife– A wife with superhuman oral sex powers.
*Looks to Heavens– With head titled towards the sky seeking a godly answer.
*Wife'ism– Wife Lifestyle.

Page 7

*Locals- Everybody who isn't famous or seriously rich.

**Wave- The vibe in which one chooses to enjoy their life.

*HollyHood- Celebrities that do normal people stuff but don't want normal people to know how normal they are.

**Gems- Knowledge

*More wives knowest than not- Majority of married women know and allow their husbands go outside of the marriage.

**How U Doin?- How you like that news. (Tagline for Wendy Williams, see REFRENCES)

Page 9

**Starter Kit- A variety of tools one needs to pursue someone or something.

Page 10

**Conversation Piece- Something or someone that stirs people to talk and or discus that subject. A hot topic.

**Woke- When the mind reaches a higher level of overstanding through self-knowledge/world knowledge and cultural knowledge.

**Shade- Subliminally make a passive aggressive statement or action.

**D'Usse- A cognac. Dark alcoholic beverage made at Chateau De Cognac in France.

**Patron- A tequila handcrafted from100% Weber Blue Agave by Patron Spirits Company.

Page 15
*Wife Life- The daily lifestyle of a married woman.
**Close Mouth Don't Get Fed- to get what you want you have to let someone know what you need.
Page 20
*Throw A Battery in Your Back- A harsh piece of information that uses a negative made up scenario that motivates positive action or thought. A harsh example of the reality and severity of things.
Page 21
**Homies- Close friends.
**Dick Pics- Pictures men send to women of there privates. A cluster of pictures of penises that women share.
**STFU- Shut the Fuck Up
**Periodt- A harsh way to say point blank. No excuses
Page 23
*Three-Legged Creature- A man with an extremely large penis. A very well-hung man.
Page 24
**OMG- Oh My God! A term used to express sudden shock.
*Tilts Head- A gesture made by leaning the head slightly towards the shoulders. A gesture that expresses uncertainty.
**Smile- Mouth Closed
Page 25
*Histress- A man dealing with a married woman.
Page 26
**WTF- What the Fuck.
Page 31

Madden 2k- A game that grown men will die for.

Cooch- Vagina.

Wenches- Young women or a girl.

Page 32

Get With The Shits- Get on board. Follow suit.

*SistaLadiFriend- Sister/Lady/Friend. A woman that wears many hats, has many trades and is very skilled. A woman that is a pillar within her community.

Dowry- Property or money offered to the husband from the family of his future bride. Wealth transferred from the wife's family to the husband's family.

*Blackness- Independent and strong in a cultural godly way.

Page 35

Naw- No with a southern accent.

*Questionable Intentions- When one starts to wonder about the motive behind one's actions, thought or through behavior.

Page 37

Hoe Is Life- A mindset to live a promiscuous lifestyle.

Sucking Him Off- Oral sex act performed on a man's penis.

*I Didn't Let the Snake Bite My Tongue- I spoke up quickly. To speak with confidence and without hesitation.

Bihh- Passive aggressive way to say bitch.

MuthaFkin Tied- Mother/Fuckin/Tired. Tired to the point of insanity. Brain in state of mush. When nothing matters. Not caring just giving it to god.

Page 38
*Stacks on Racks- Millionaire Money.
**IJS- I'm Just Saying. Passive – Aggressive ending salutation to downplay what one just said.
Page 43
**Shoot Your Shot- Take a chance. Go for it. The act of trying to get one's attention for whatever reason.
**Hoe'ism- The promiscuity Lifestyle.
Page 45
*Hoeing- Ungodly acts of sex within the promiscuity lifestyle.
**Sis- A term used by black people within their culture towards people that are not their blood sister.
Page 47
**Cheese- A open smile showing most teeth.
*Sips Jack- Just a touch of Jack Daniels whiskey to wet the throat in between sentences.
*TahDay- Today. Right now, at this moment in time. All day.
Page 48
**Twitter-Fingers- When a person takes to the internet in a mad frenzy to express their thoughts without caring to spell/grammar check.
**LMAO- Laughing My Ass Off. Really Funny. Laughing to the point of releasing gas from the anus.
**WTF- Who the Fuck
Page 52

**Do You- Do what's in the best interest of self. An action one takes without the consideration of others.
**Lort- A black person who is putting emphasis on God without going to hell.

THE HAPPY MISTRESS
VOL. II
SECRETS OF A HAPPY
WIFE

The movies, places, people, or things that helped this volume take off. I guess you would call them⋯ REFERENCES

Page 7
WENDY WILLIAMS– American Day Time, Talk Show Host mainly gossip and big news within the entertainment world.
Page 8
Mrs.Harris– Tiny Harris, Wife of Southern American Rap Artist/Actor "T.I."
T.I.– Tip Harris, Rap Artist/Actor based from/in Atlanta, GA.
Page 38
Secrets of A Happy Mistress– Volume I to this book. Book One.
Page 42
Marriage, Men & Mistresses– A panel series starting in 2020 discussing the views men have on Marriage, & Mistresses.
Hilliard Clinton– Wife of 42cd President of The United States. Former 1st Lady.
Bill Clinton– 42cd President of The United States.
Page 44
Players Club– Movie produced by American based Rapper, "Ice Cube", in 1998 about the lifestyle of strippers and the strip club.
Shug Avery– Character in the American Movie, "The Color Purple".

The Color Purple- An American Movie produced by," Quincy Jones" about the life of character, "Celie".

Prince- Great International R&B Icon.

She Devil- 1989 Screenplay about a woman who tries to put up with her husband's infidelity. After getting mad she gets revenge.

Rosanne Barr- American actress that played in the American movie; "She Devil".

Page 47

Mr. Mom- American Movie based on a comedy about a dad that takes on his wife's duties including mom duties.

Page 52

Elizabeth Taylor- American Icon. Actress. Known for the number of husbands she wed, her good looks and expensive taste.

Where Can You Find the Author, Noella Fe?

Where in the heck can you find me? Look below, I have a whole list of places! Pick your Poison! Wanna discuss the book or have questions? Email me anytime @
noellafesays@gmail.com
Questions about publications or booking Noella Fe at your next panel? Email the team@
sistaladifriend@gmail.com
Would you like to know about upcoming book releases and events? Subscribe to our website @ Sistaladifriend.com
Want to win free books or join our book club? Follow our facebook page @
SistaLadiFriend Publishing Company/ FB
Want to see Noella Fe in action, follow our Instagram post for the best photos, captions and inspirational quotes @
Sistaladifriend/IG

www.ingramcontent.com/pod-product-compliance
Lightning Source LLC
LaVergne TN
LVHW051421080426
835508LV00022B/3187